WE CAN
AND WE WILL
BEST TEAM
EVER

Date: /   /

_____

_____

_____

_____

_____

_____

_____

_____

_____

_____

_____

_____

_____

_____

_____

_____

_____

_____

_____

_____

_____

_____

THINGS TO BE GRATEFUL FOR TODAY

"Have dreams and dream big! Dream without fear"

Date: ___ / ___ / ___

_____

_____

_____

_____

_____

_____

_____

_____

_____

_____

_____

_____

_____

_____

_____

_____

_____

_____

_____

_____

THINGS TO BE GRATEFUL FOR TODAY

Date: /   /

THINGS TO BE GRATEFUL FOR TODAY

> *"They say I dream too big. I say they think too small"* - Unknown

Date: /   /

THINGS TO BE GRATEFUL FOR TODAY

> *"Never be afraid to start something new,*
> *if you fail it is just temporary, if you believe*
> *and persist you will succeed"*

Date: /   /

THINGS TO BE GRATEFUL FOR TODAY

Date: /   /

_____

_____

_____

_____

_____

_____

_____

_____

_____

_____

_____

_____

_____

_____

_____

_____

_____

_____

_____

THINGS TO BE GRATEFUL FOR TODAY

> *"Wherever you go, go with all your heart."*
> *- Confucius*

Date: /   /

_____
_____
_____
_____
_____
_____
_____
_____
_____
_____
_____
_____
_____
_____
_____
_____
_____
_____
_____
_____

THINGS TO BE GRATEFUL FOR TODAY

"Never Ever Give Up"

Date: /   /

_____

_____

_____

_____

_____

_____

_____

_____

_____

_____

_____

_____

_____

_____

_____

_____

_____

_____

_____

_____

_____

THINGS TO BE GRATEFUL FOR TODAY

"Start where you are and take chances"

Date: /   /

THINGS TO BE GRATEFUL FOR TODAY

"keep taking chances - make life a beautiful experience and never give up"

Date: /   /

_____

_____

_____

_____

_____

_____

_____

_____

_____

_____

_____

_____

_____

_____

_____

_____

_____

THINGS TO BE GRATEFUL FOR TODAY

"Life isn't about finding yourself. Life is about creating yourself." - George Bernard Shaw

Date: /   /

THINGS TO BE GRATEFUL FOR TODAY

"Change your life today. Don't gamble on the future, act now, without delay." — Simone de Beauvoir

Date: /   /

_____

_____

_____

_____

_____

_____

_____

_____

_____

_____

_____

_____

_____

_____

_____

_____

_____

_____

_____

THINGS TO BE GRATEFUL FOR TODAY

Date: /   /

THINGS TO BE GRATEFUL FOR TODAY

"Aim for the stars to keep your dreams alive"

Date: /   /

_____

_____

_____

_____

_____

_____

_____

_____

_____

_____

_____

_____

_____

_____

_____

_____

_____

_____

THINGS TO BE GRATEFUL FOR TODAY

"When life gives you lemons, add a little gin and tonic"

Date: /   /

_____

_____

_____

_____

_____

_____

_____

_____

_____

_____

_____

_____

_____

_____

_____

_____

_____

_____

THINGS TO BE GRATEFUL FOR TODAY

Date: /   /

THINGS TO BE GRATEFUL FOR TODAY

"Opportunity comes to those who never give up"

Date: /   /

_____

_____

_____

_____

_____

_____

_____

_____

_____

_____

_____

_____

_____

_____

_____

_____

_____

_____

_____

_____

_____

THINGS TO BE GRATEFUL FOR TODAY

Date: /   /

THINGS TO BE GRATEFUL FOR TODAY

Date: /   /

THINGS TO BE GRATEFUL FOR TODAY

> *"Success is not a place or a destination, it is a way of thinking while always having a new goal in mind"*

Date: /   /

_____

_____
_____
_____
_____
_____
_____
_____
_____
_____
_____
_____
_____
_____
_____
_____
_____
_____

THINGS TO BE GRATEFUL FOR TODAY

*"Every achievement starts with
a dream and a goal in mind"*

Date: /   /

THINGS TO BE GRATEFUL FOR TODAY

> *"Change the world one dream at a time,*
> *believe in your dreams"*

Date: /   /

_____
_____
_____
_____
_____
_____
_____
_____
_____
_____
_____
_____
_____
_____
_____
_____
_____
_____
_____
_____

THINGS TO BE GRATEFUL FOR TODAY

> *"Never loose confidence in your dreams,*
> *there will be obstacles and defeats, but you will*
> *always win if you persist"*

Date: /   /

THINGS TO BE GRATEFUL FOR TODAY

""Never wait for someone else to validate your existence, you are the creator of your own destiny"

Date: /   /

THINGS TO BE GRATEFUL FOR TODAY

"Dreams are the energy that power your life"

Date: /   /

THINGS TO BE GRATEFUL FOR TODAY

"Dreams make things happen, nothing is impossible as long as you believe." - Anonymous

Date: /   /
_____

_____
_____
_____
_____
_____
_____
_____
_____
_____
_____
_____
_____
_____
_____
_____
_____
_____
_____

THINGS TO BE GRATEFUL FOR TODAY

"Always dream big and follow your heart"

Date: /   /

THINGS TO BE GRATEFUL FOR TODAY

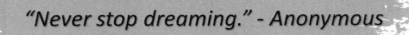

"Never stop dreaming." - Anonymous

Date: /   /

THINGS TO BE GRATEFUL FOR TODAY

Date: /   /

THINGS TO BE GRATEFUL FOR TODAY

"Dream big, it's the first step to success" - Anonymous

Date: /   /

_____
_____
_____
_____
_____
_____
_____
_____
_____
_____
_____
_____
_____
_____
_____
_____
_____
_____
_____
_____

THINGS TO BE GRATEFUL FOR TODAY

"A successful person is someone that understands temporary defeat as a learning process, never give up!"

Date: /   /

THINGS TO BE GRATEFUL FOR TODAY

> *"Motivation comes from working on our dreams and from taking action to achieve our goals"*

Date: /   /

_____

_____

_____

_____

_____

_____

_____

_____

_____

_____

_____

_____

_____

_____

_____

_____

_____

_____

_____

THINGS TO BE GRATEFUL FOR TODAY

> *"Dreams are the foundation to our imagination and success"*

Date: /   /

THINGS TO BE GRATEFUL FOR TODAY

Date: /   /

THINGS TO BE GRATEFUL FOR TODAY

"Doing what you believe in, and going after your dreams will only result in success." - Anonymous

Date: /   /

_____

_____

_____

_____

_____

_____

_____

_____

_____

_____

_____

_____

_____

_____

_____

_____

_____

_____

_____

_____

_____

THINGS TO BE GRATEFUL FOR TODAY

"The right time to start something new is now"

Date: /   /

THINGS TO BE GRATEFUL FOR TODAY

> *"Be brave, fight for what you believe in and make your dreams a reality."* - Anonymous

Date: /   /

_____

_____

_____

_____

_____

_____

_____

_____

_____

_____

_____

_____

_____

_____

_____

_____

_____

_____

_____

_____

THINGS TO BE GRATEFUL FOR TODAY

Date: /   /

_____

_____

_____

_____

_____

_____

_____

_____

_____

_____

_____

_____

_____

_____

_____

_____

_____

_____

_____

THINGS TO BE GRATEFUL FOR TODAY

"Let your dreams be bigger than your fears and your actions louder than your words." - Anonymous

Date: /   /

_____
_____
_____
_____
_____
_____
_____
_____
_____
_____
_____
_____
_____
_____
_____
_____
_____
_____
_____
_____
_____

THINGS TO BE GRATEFUL FOR TODAY

"Always keep moving forward to keep your balance, if you stop dreaming you will fall"

Date: /   /

THINGS TO BE GRATEFUL FOR TODAY

Date: /   /

THINGS TO BE GRATEFUL FOR TODAY

"Dream. Believe. Create. Succeed" - Anonymous

Date: /   /

THINGS TO BE GRATEFUL FOR TODAY

> *"You are never to old to set new goals and achieve them, keep on dreaming!"*

Date: /   /

THINGS TO BE GRATEFUL FOR TODAY

Date: /   /

_____

_____

_____

_____

_____

_____

_____

_____

_____

_____

_____

_____

_____

_____

_____

_____

_____

_____

_____

THINGS TO BE GRATEFUL FOR TODAY

"Difficulties are nothing more than opportunities in disguise, keep on trying and you will succeed"

Date: /   /

THINGS TO BE GRATEFUL FOR TODAY

> *"To achieve our dreams we must first overcome our fear of failure"*

Date: /   /

THINGS TO BE GRATEFUL FOR TODAY

"Always have a powerful reason to wake up every new morning, set goals and follow your dreams"

Date: /   /

_____

_____

_____

_____

_____

_____

_____

_____

_____

_____

_____

_____

_____

_____

_____

_____

_____

_____

THINGS TO BE GRATEFUL FOR TODAY

"Use failure as a motivation tool not as a sign of defeat"

Date: /   /

_____

_____

_____

_____

_____

_____

_____

_____

_____

_____

_____

_____

_____

_____

_____

_____

_____

_____

_____

THINGS TO BE GRATEFUL FOR TODAY

> *"Never let your dreams die for fear of failure,*
> *defeat is just temporary; your dreams are your power"*

Date: /   /

_____

_____

_____

_____

_____

_____

_____

_____

_____

_____

_____

_____

_____

_____

_____

_____

_____

_____

_____

THINGS TO BE GRATEFUL FOR TODAY

> *"A failure is a lesson, not a loss. It is a temporary and sometimes necessary detour, not a dead end"*

Date: /   /

_____

_____

_____

_____

_____

_____

_____

_____

_____

_____

_____

_____

_____

_____

_____

_____

_____

_____

_____

_____

THINGS TO BE GRATEFUL FOR TODAY

"Have faith in the future but above all in yourself"

Date: /   /

_____

_____

_____

_____

_____

_____

_____

_____

_____

_____

_____

_____

_____

_____

_____

_____

_____

_____

_____

THINGS TO BE GRATEFUL FOR TODAY

Date: /   /

THINGS TO BE GRATEFUL FOR TODAY

> *"Your future is created by what you do today not tomorrow"* - Anonymous

Date: /   /

THINGS TO BE GRATEFUL FOR TODAY

"Never let your doubt blind your goals, for your future lies in your ability, not your failure" — Anonymous

Date: /   /

_____
_____
_____
_____
_____
_____
_____
_____
_____
_____
_____
_____
_____
_____
_____
_____
_____
_____
_____

THINGS TO BE GRATEFUL FOR TODAY

> *"Don't go into something to test the waters, go into things to make waves"* — Anonymous

Date: / /

_____

THINGS TO BE GRATEFUL FOR TODAY

> *"Laughter is the shock absorber that softens and minimizes the bumps of life"* — *Anonymous*

Date: /   /
_____

_____
_____
_____
_____
_____
_____
_____
_____
_____
_____
_____
_____
_____
_____
_____
_____
_____
_____

THINGS TO BE GRATEFUL FOR TODAY

Date: /   /

THINGS TO BE GRATEFUL FOR TODAY

"Make your own destiny. Don't wait for it to come to you, life is not a rehearsal" — Anonymous

Date: /   /

THINGS TO BE GRATEFUL FOR TODAY

"If you want to feel rich, just count all the things you have that money can't buy" — *Anonymous*

Date: /   /

THINGS TO BE GRATEFUL FOR TODAY

> *"Never give up on a dream just because of the time it will take to accomplish it. The time will pass anyway."* — *Anonymous*

Date: /   /

THINGS TO BE GRATEFUL FOR TODAY

"I am never a failure until I begin blaming others"
- Anonymous

Date: /   /

THINGS TO BE GRATEFUL FOR TODAY

"Your only limitation is your imagination" — Anonymous

Date: /   /
_____
_____
_____
_____
_____
_____
_____
_____
_____
_____
_____
_____
_____
_____
_____
_____
_____
_____
_____
_____
_____

THINGS TO BE GRATEFUL FOR TODAY

> *"Some pursue success and happiness – others create it"* — Anonymous

Date: /   /

THINGS TO BE GRATEFUL FOR TODAY

Date: /   /

THINGS TO BE GRATEFUL FOR TODAY

> *"It's better to have an impossible dream than no dream at all."* — Anonymous

Date: /   /

_____

_____

_____

_____

_____

_____

_____

_____

_____

_____

_____

_____

_____

_____

_____

_____

_____

_____

_____

THINGS TO BE GRATEFUL FOR TODAY

"Never let defeat have the last word" — Anonymous

Date: /   /

_____

_____

_____

_____

_____

_____

_____

_____

_____

_____

_____

_____

_____

_____

_____

_____

_____

_____

_____

THINGS TO BE GRATEFUL FOR TODAY

> *"The winner always has a plan; The loser always has an excuse"* — Anonymous

Date: /   /

_____
_____
_____
_____
_____
_____
_____
_____
_____
_____
_____
_____
_____
_____
_____
_____
_____
_____
_____
_____
_____

THINGS TO BE GRATEFUL FOR TODAY

Date: /   /

_____

_____

_____

_____

_____

_____

_____

_____

_____

_____

_____

_____

_____

_____

_____

_____

_____

_____

THINGS TO BE GRATEFUL FOR TODAY

"Don't let yesterday's disappointments, overshadow tomorrow's achievements" — Anonymous

Date: /   /

THINGS TO BE GRATEFUL FOR TODAY

"We are limited, not by our abilities, but by our vision"
— Anonymous

Date: /   /

THINGS TO BE GRATEFUL FOR TODAY

"Dreams don't come true. Dreams are true"
— Anonymous

Date: /   /

THINGS TO BE GRATEFUL FOR TODAY

> *"Happiness is not something you get,*
> *but something you do"* — *Anonymous*

Date: /   /

_____

_____

_____

_____

_____

_____

_____

_____

_____

_____

_____

_____

_____

_____

_____

_____

_____

_____

_____

THINGS TO BE GRATEFUL FOR TODAY

D   Date: /

THINGS TO BE GRATEFUL FOR TODAY

Date: /   /

_____
_____
_____
_____
_____
_____
_____
_____
_____
_____
_____
_____
_____
_____
_____
_____
_____
_____
_____

THINGS TO BE GRATEFUL FOR TODAY

> *"No dreamer is ever too small; no dream is ever too big." – Anonymous*

Date: /   /

_____

_____

_____

_____

_____

_____

_____

_____

_____

_____

_____

_____

_____

_____

_____

_____

_____

_____

THINGS TO BE GRATEFUL FOR TODAY

"All our tomorrows depend on today" — *Anonymous*

Date: /   /

THINGS TO BE GRATEFUL FOR TODAY

Date: /   /

THINGS TO BE GRATEFUL FOR TODAY

"Dream is not what you see in sleep, dream is the thing which does not let you sleep" — Anonymous

Date: / /

_____
_____
_____
_____
_____
_____
_____
_____
_____
_____
_____
_____
_____
_____
_____
_____
_____
_____
_____

THINGS TO BE GRATEFUL FOR TODAY

Date: /   /

THINGS TO BE GRATEFUL FOR TODAY

> *"Dreams give purpose to your life and meaning to your existence"*

Date: /   /

_____

_____

_____

_____

_____

_____

_____

_____

_____

_____

_____

_____

_____

_____

_____

_____

_____

_____

THINGS TO BE GRATEFUL FOR TODAY

Date: /   /

THINGS TO BE GRATEFUL FOR TODAY

"Follow your heart and your dreams will come true"
– Anonymous

Date: /   /

THINGS TO BE GRATEFUL FOR TODAY

"You create your life by following your dreams with decisive actions"

Date: /   /

THINGS TO BE GRATEFUL FOR TODAY

> *"Without dreams you lose interest in life, you have no energy to move forward"*

Date: /   /

_____
_____
_____
_____
_____
_____
_____
_____
_____
_____
_____
_____
_____
_____
_____
_____
_____
_____
_____

THINGS TO BE GRATEFUL FOR TODAY

"Difficult roads often lead to beautiful destinations"

Date: /   /

THINGS TO BE GRATEFUL FOR TODAY

Date: /   /

_____

_____

_____

_____

_____

_____

_____

_____

_____

_____

_____

_____

_____

_____

_____

_____

_____

_____

_____

THINGS TO BE GRATEFUL FOR TODAY

"Believe in yourself and you will be unstoppable"

Date: /   /

_____
_____
_____
_____
_____
_____
_____
_____
_____
_____
_____
_____
_____
_____
_____
_____
_____
_____
_____
_____
_____
_____
_____

THINGS TO BE GRATEFUL FOR TODAY

Date: /   /

THINGS TO BE GRATEFUL FOR TODAY

"To live a creative life, we must lose our fear of being wrong" - Anonymous

Date: /   /

THINGS TO BE GRATEFUL FOR TODAY

> *"Make each day count, you will never have this day again"*

Date: /   /

_____

_____

_____

_____

_____

_____

_____

_____

_____

_____

_____

_____

_____

_____

_____

_____

_____

THINGS TO BE GRATEFUL FOR TODAY

> *"If you do what you always did,*
> *you will get what you always got" - Anonymous*

Date: /   /

THINGS TO BE GRATEFUL FOR TODAY

Date: /   /

_____

_____

_____

_____

_____

_____

_____

_____

_____

_____

_____

_____

_____

_____

_____

_____

_____

THINGS TO BE GRATEFUL FOR TODAY

"You are capable of amazing things"

Date: /   /

THINGS TO BE GRATEFUL FOR TODAY

"Believe in yourself and you will be unstoppable"

Date: /   /

_____

_____

_____

_____

_____

_____

_____

_____

_____

_____

_____

_____

_____

_____

_____

_____

_____

_____

_____

_____

THINGS TO BE GRATEFUL FOR TODAY

Date: /   /

THINGS TO BE GRATEFUL FOR TODAY

Date: /   /

THINGS TO BE GRATEFUL FOR TODAY

"Nothing worth having comes easy" - Anonymous

Date: /   /

_____

_____

_____

_____

_____

_____

_____

_____

_____

_____

_____

_____

_____

_____

_____

_____

_____

THINGS TO BE GRATEFUL FOR TODAY

"Follow your dreams, they know the way"

Date: /   /

THINGS TO BE GRATEFUL FOR TODAY

"Don't Let Anyone Dull Your Sparkle"

Date: /   /

THINGS TO BE GRATEFUL FOR TODAY

CREATIVE JOURNALS FACTORY

We hope you liked your journal – notebook, please let us know if you liked it by writing a review, it means a lot to us.

Thank you!

DESIGNED BY POSITIVE GIFTS PRESS FOR:

CREATIVE JOURNALS FACTORY

FIND OTHER BEAUTIFUL JOURNALS, DIARIES AND NOTEBOOKS AT:

www.CreativeJournalsFactory.com

JOURNALS - DIARIES - NOTEBOOKS - COLORING BOOKS